Pennworthy 514111 428.99

SCOOBY-DOO!

A SCIENCE OF LIGHT MYSTERY

by Megan Cooley Peterson

illustrated by Dario Brizuela

THE ANGRY ALIEN

CAPSTONE PRESS

a capstone imprint

Scooby-Doo and the gang drove home from a day at the beach.

"Man, all that sand and sun sure make a person hungry," Shaggy said.

"Rungry," Scooby-Doo agreed.

"There might be some sandwiches left in the cooler," Velma said.

"I wish it weren't so dark tonight," Shaggy said. "I can't see what I'm doing! Good thing I can smell a sandwich from a mile away!"

"And I can't see anything," Daphne said. "Not even the road!" She slammed on the brakes.

"Like, who turned out the lights?" Shaggy asked.

"The van's headlights must have burned out," Fred said.

"There's a town up the road," Velma said. "Maybe we can find a repair shop."

"And something to eat," added Shaggy, rubbing his stomach. "Someone ate all the sandwiches."

"Those woods look awfully creepy," Daphne whispered.

"It's a good thing we have these flashlights," Fred said. "Or we'd be walking in total darkness."

"Like, how do we make light, anyway?" Shaggy asked.

"Light is a kind of energy," Velma explained. "A unit of light is called a photon. Photons are like tiny packets of energy."

"Velma's right," said Fred. "Photons travel together in light waves."

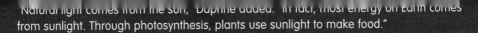

"Natural light comes from the sun," Daphne added. "In fact, most energy on Earth comes from sunlight. Through photosynthesis, plants use sunlight to make food."

"Are you telling me that I have light to thank for French fries?" Shaggy asked.

"Yep," Velma said. "Light feeds plants. Plants feed plant-eating animals. And plant-eating animals feed the meat-eaters. Without the sun and its light, there would be no life on Earth."

"And what kind of light would that be?" Shaggy asked, pointing at the sky.

"It looks like a UFO!" shouted Fred.

FACT FILE

Light travels about 1,000 feet (305 meters) in one-millionth of a second. It takes about eight minutes for light to reach Earth from the sun.

5

"That UFO disappeared into thin air," Daphne said. "How strange."

"Strange, indeed," agreed Velma. "Maybe someone in town will be able to explain what's going on."

"I hope we don't run into any aliens," Shaggy added.

"Raliens?" asked Scooby.

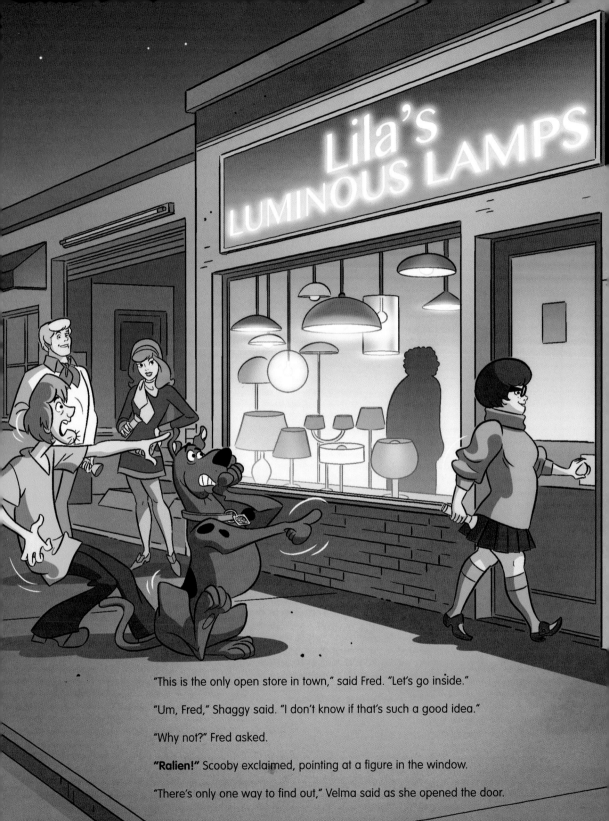

"This is the only open store in town," said Fred. "Let's go inside."

"Um, Fred," Shaggy said. "I don't know if that's such a good idea."

"Why not?" Fred asked.

"Ralien!" Scooby exclaimed, pointing at a figure in the window.

"There's only one way to find out," Velma said as she opened the door.

"Whew! We, like, thought you were an alien," Shaggy said to the store owner.

"I'm no alien. I'm Lila," the woman said. "Can I interest you kids in a new lamp?"

"Actually," Fred said, "our van broke down. But the repair shop is closed."

Shaggy put on his sunglasses. "This is one bright store you have here," he said. "I guess all light doesn't come from the sun."

"All natural light comes from the sun," Velma said. "But light bulbs use electricity to make light."

"Velma's right," said Daphne. "Inside an incandescent light bulb is a tiny wire called a filament. When electricity passes through the filament, it heats up and glows by releasing photons."

"But incandescent bulbs produce a lot of unwanted heat along with the light. They waste more energy than other types of light bulbs," Velma added.

"Look, Scoob! It's a shadow alien," Shaggy said.

"I wouldn't joke about aliens," Lila said. "They've been scaring away my customers."

"We thought we saw a UFO just outside of town," Velma said. "Do you know anything about it?"

"All I know is business has been terrible lately because of alien sightings nearby," Lila said. "There's a storage room in the back you can sleep in if you need a place to stay."

FACT FILE

Many inventors experimented with incandescent light bulbs. Thomas Edison invented the most successful incandescent bulb in 1879. For many years, Edison's bulb was the only kind commonly used. Today people tend to choose more energy-efficient options. CFL and LED light bulbs last longer and waste less energy.

"Man, this storage room is creepier than the UFO," Shaggy observed.

"You heard what Lila said about the aliens. Something strange is going on in this town," Velma said.

"Looks like we've got another mystery to solve, gang," Fred added.

"How am I supposed to solve a mystery on an empty stomach?" Shaggy asked.

"Rook! Ralien!" Scooby shouted.

"That's not an alien," Fred said. "It's your reflection, Scoob."

"Reflection?" Scooby asked.

"Light waves move in a straight line," Daphne explained. "When light hits an object, it is absorbed or reflected. It can also pass through certain objects, like glass."

"When you look in a mirror, some light bounces off your face," said Velma. "That light hits the mirror."

"Most household mirrors are made of sheets of glass backed with metal," added Fred. "The light passes through the glass. It bounces off the metal and into your eyes."

"Oh, look," Shaggy said, pointing to the window. "There's someone outside carrying two flashlights."

"Those aren't flashlights," Fred said.

"They're glowing **alien eyeballs**!" exclaimed Daphne.

"Let's go investigate!" Velma suggested.

"Man, that alien is faster than the Mystery Machine," panted Shaggy. "We tried to catch it, but it disappeared into the woods."

"Rast ralien," agreed Scooby.

"Something, or someone, tampered with this electrical box," Velma noticed. "The electricity's been cut off."

"And there's a pile of screws lying on the ground," added Fred. "Our first clue!"

"I hope the next clue leads us to a plate of cheeseburgers with extra ketchup," muttered Shaggy.

"What happened to your lamps?" Fred asked Lila the next morning. "We didn't hear a thing over Shaggy's loud snoring."

"I told you—it's the alien! It broke all these lamps and stole dozens more," said Lila.

"Like, why would an alien want a bunch of lamps?" asked Shaggy.

"It must be using lamp parts to build another UFO," Lila guessed.

"Look!" Daphne said. "Scooby found more screws."

"Do you know anything about these screws?" Velma asked. "We found some near your broken electrical box."

Lila shrugged. "They don't look familiar to me."

"Let's walk back to the van and drive it to the repair shop," Fred said. "We can ask if the mechanic knows what happened."

"Do you know anything about the alien that vandalized the lamp store?" Velma asked the mechanic later that morning.

"Aliens don't exist," the mechanic scoffed.

"Rook!" said Scooby. "Rews!"

"Don't touch those screws," said the mechanic. "I'm almost out, and my next order won't get here until next week."

"Zoinks!" Shaggy pointed to a strange light on the wall. "The alien is, like, playing tricks on my eyes—I'm seeing rainbows!"

"The rainbow isn't from an alien," said the mechanic. "It's coming from my daughter, Iris."

"Like, whew," said Shaggy. "But I've never seen a magic rock that can make rainbows."

"This is a prism," Iris said. "Prisms cause light refraction."

"Is refraction anything like subtraction? I'm not so good at math," said Shaggy.

Iris smiled. "No, it's science. Refraction is when light waves bend. I've been studying light at school. It's my favorite science topic."

"So, like, does a prism make colors?" Shaggy asked.

"Not exactly," Fred said. "Visible light looks white to us, but it is actually made of all colors. Each color has a different wavelength."

"Each wavelength bends at a different angle as it passes through the prism," Velma continued. "The prism separates the different wavelengths, or colors, so a rainbow appears."

"Refraction isn't the only way we see colors," said Daphne. "A tomato looks red because it reflects only red light. It absorbs all the other colors."

"Black objects absorb most colors," added Fred. "And white objects reflect all the colors."

"There's even more to light than refraction and wavelengths," Iris said. "Let me show you our solar panels."

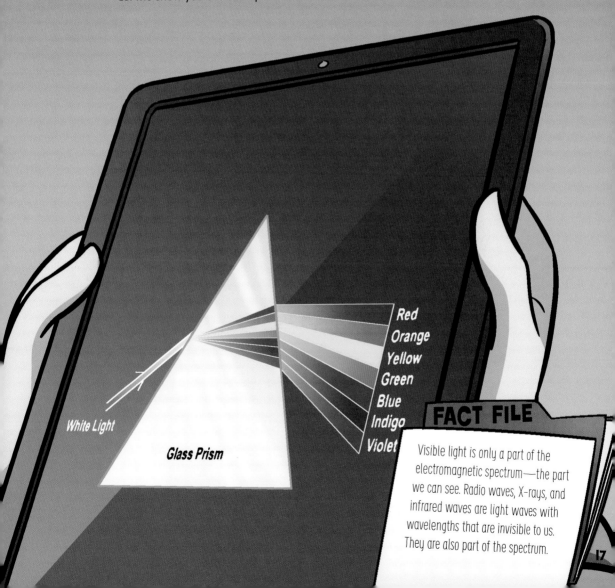

White Light

Glass Prism

Red
Orange
Yellow
Green
Blue
Indigo
Violet

FACT FILE

Visible light is only a part of the electromagnetic spectrum—the part we can see. Radio waves, X-rays, and infrared waves are light waves with wavelengths that are invisible to us. They are also part of the spectrum.

"I convinced my mom to install these solar panels," said Iris. "Pretty cool, huh?"

Velma nodded. "When sunlight hits the solar panels, photons bump into electrons. The electrons break free from the atoms and create a flow of electricity."

"Solar power is better for the environment than burning fossil fuels," said Fred.

"I've been trying to get the whole town to switch to solar power," Iris said. "But so far, no one will cooperate."

"There's something shady about that mechanic and those screws that keep turning up," Velma said.

"Let's come back tonight," Fred suggested.

Scooby's stomach growled. "Rungry," he said.

"Scooby and I are, like, totally on the same wavelength. Let's get some pizza!" Shaggy said.

That night the gang headed back to the repair shop. "Like, what are these funky sunglasses for?" Shaggy asked. "They're turning everything green!"

"They're not sunglasses," explained Daphne. "They're night-vision goggles."

"These goggles collect all the available light, including the light we can't see," said Fred. "They change photons of light energy into electrons. The electrons multiply. When the electrons hit a special screen, they change back into photons."

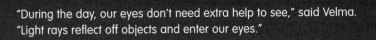

"During the day, our eyes don't need extra help to see," said Velma. "Light rays reflect off objects and enter our eyes."

"The iris controls how much light enters the eye," continued Fred. "The light creates an image on the retina. And the retina sends the image to the brain."

"The reflected light tells your eyes the object is there," added Daphne. "Without light, we wouldn't be able to see anything around us."

FACT FILE

The image projected onto the retina is actually upside down. Our brains turn the image right side up.

"**Look!**" Daphne shouted. "The alien! It's running toward the woods!"

"**After it, gang!**" said Fred.

"Look what Scoob found! How does the alien fly in such a tiny spacecraft?" asked Shaggy.

"Not so fast," said Fred. "It's a toy helicopter. Someone made it look like a UFO."

"I found Iris's prism in the grass," Shaggy said. "What's it doing out here?"

"It's time to shine some light on this mystery," said Daphne.

Shaggy gulped. "I was afraid you'd say that."

"Shaggy, why are you and Scooby wearing costumes?" asked Velma.

"If you can't beat 'em, join 'em, I say," said Shaggy. "Maybe the alien will share some space snacks with us?"

"Let's try to lure the alien using this spotlight," said Fred.

"And then we'll drop this net on it," added Daphne.

"So, like, does this spotlight have superpowers to make it so bright?" asked Shaggy.

"The light bulb makes light," Velma said. "The area around the bulb reflects the light, making it even brighter. It also angles the light upward to create a strong beam."

"**Zoinks! It worked!**" shouted Shaggy.

"What's going on?" the mechanic asked, joining the group.

"We caught the alien!" Velma said. "Time to see who, or what, it really is." Scooby peeled off the alien's mask.

"Iris?" said her mother.

"Rews!" Scooby said, pointing to the tiny horns on the alien's mask.

"Like, I think we solved the alien mystery, and the mystery of the missing screws," Shaggy said.

"I've been trying to scare Lila into using energy efficient options like LED bulbs in her store. But she won't listen to me!" said Iris.

"So you broke her lamps and tampered with the electrical box," said Daphne.

"And I would have gotten away with it if it weren't for you meddling out-of-towners!" said Iris.

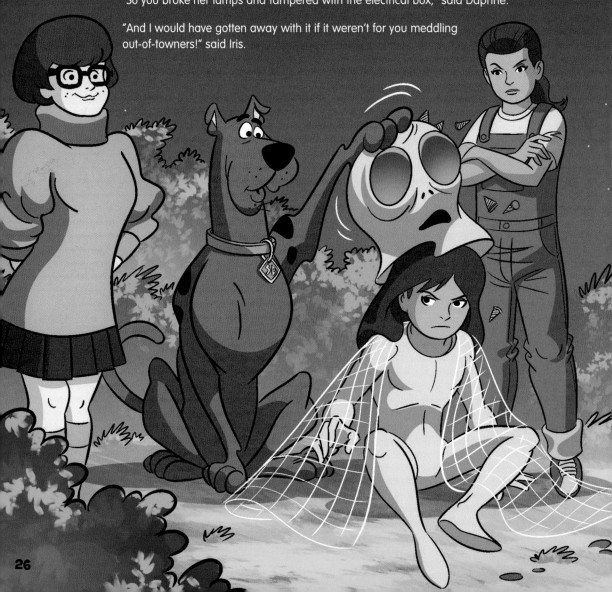

"Well, gang, it looks like our work here is done," said Fred.

"Not quite," said Shaggy. "We have one more mystery to solve."

"What's that?" asked Velma.

"The mystery of where to find some out-of-this-world cheeseburgers!" Shaggy said.

"Hee hee hee!" Scooby giggled and licked his lips.

THE END

GLOSSARY

atom (AT-uhm)—the smallest particle of an element

CFL—a bulb that produces light when electricity flows through a tube filled with a type of gas; CFL is short for compact fluorescent light

electricity (i-lek-TRIS-i-tee)—a flow of electrons that can be used to make light and heat or to make machines work

electron (i-LEK-tron)—a tiny particle in an atom that travels around the nucleus

fossil fuels (FAH-suhl FYOOLZ)—natural fuels formed from the remains of plants and animals; coal, oil, and natural gas are fossil fuels

incandescent bulb (in-kuhn-DES-uhnt buhlb)—a bulb that lights up when electricity heats its filament causing it to glow

infrared (in-fruh-RED)—invisible light that is next to red in the rainbow

LED—an LED is an electronic device that emits light when a voltage is applied to it; LED is short for light-emitting diode

photon (FOH-ton)—a particle or unit of light

radio waves (RAY-dee-oh WAYV)—invisible low-energy light that is used for radio and TV

reflection (ri-FLEK-shun)—the change in direction of light bouncing off a surface

refraction (ri-FRAKT-shun)—the bending of light; light is refracted when it travels through a prism or a lens

retina (RET-uhn-uh)—the lining inside the back of the eyeball

solar power (SOH-lur POU-ur)—energy from the sun that can be used for heating and electricity

wavelength (WAYV-length)—the distance between two peaks of a wave

X-ray (EKS-ray)—invisible high-energy light that can pass through solid objects

SCIENCE AND ENGINEERING PRACTICES

1. Asking questions (for science) and defining problems (for engineering)

2. Developing and using models

3. Planning and carrying out investigations

4. Analyzing and interpreting data

5. Using mathematics and computational thinking

6. Constructing explanations (for science) and designing solutions (for engineering)

7. Engaging in argument from evidence

8. Obtaining, evaluating, and communicating information

Next Generation Science Standards

READ MORE

Bow, James. *Energy from the Sun: Solar Power.* Next Generation Energy. New York: Crabtree Publishing, 2016.

Dolan, Ellen M. *Thomas Alva Edison: American Inventor and Businessman.* Legendary American Biographies. Berkeley Heights, N.J.: Enslow Publishers, Inc., 2015.

Solway, Andrew. *From Sunlight to Blockbuster Movies: An Energy Journey through the World of Light.* Energy Journeys. Chicago: Capstone Heinemann Library, 2015.

INTERNET SITES

FactHound offers a safe, fun way to find Internet sites related to this book. All of the sites on FactHound have been researched by our staff.

Here's all you do:

Visit *www.facthound.com*

Type in this code: 9781515737001

Check out projects, games and lots more at
www.capstonekids.com

INDEX

Thanks to our adviser for his expertise, research, and advice:
Paul Ohmann, PhD, Associate Professor of Physics
University of St. Thomas, St. Paul, Minnesota

Published in 2017 by Capstone Press, A Capstone Imprint
1710 Roe Crest Drive, North Mankato, Minnesota 56003
www.mycapstone.com

Library of Congress Cataloging-in-Publication Data
is available on the library of congress website.
ISBN: 978-1-5157-3700-1 (library hardcover)
978-1-5157-3704-9 (paperback)
978-1-5157-3716-2 (eBook PDF)
Summary: The aliens have landed! That's what Scooby-Doo and the gang think
when they see a UFO and an alien who seems determined to destroy the local
lighting store. But why? Join the gang as they use science to uncover the
alien's mission and put a stop to its not-so-bright idea.

Editorial Credits
Editor: Kristen Mohn
Designer: Ashlee Suker
Creative Director: Nathan Gassman
Production Specialist: Laura Manthe
The illustrations in this book were created digitally.

Printed in the United States of America.
010051S17

OTHER TITLES IN THIS SET:

A SCIENCE OF CHEMICAL REACTIONS MYSTERY

A SCIENCE OF ELECTRICITY MYSTERY

A SCIENCE OF ENERGY MYSTERY

A SCIENCE OF MAGNETISM MYSTERY